Education

Alex Woolf

LUCENT BOOKS ®

THOMSON

GALE

San Diego • Detroit • New York • San Francisco • Cleveland • New Haven, Conn. • Waterville, Maine • London • Munich

THOMSON

GALE

Originally published by Hodder Wayland,
an imprint of Hodder Children's Books,
a division of Hodder Headline Limited
338 Euston Road, London NW1 3BH

For more information, contact
Lucent Books
27500 Drake Rd.
Farmington Hills, MI 48331-3535
Or you can visit our Internet site at http://www.gale.com

Design: Peta Morey
Commissioning Editor: Jane Tyler
Editor: Liz Gogerly
Picture Researcher: Glass Onion Pictures
Consultant: Malcolm Barber
Map artwork: Encompass

We are grateful to the following for permission to reproduce photographs:
The Art Archive 4, 6, 7 (bottom), 8 (top and bottom), 9, 12, 14, 17, 18, 19, 20, 21, 22, 23, 26, 27, 28, 29, 31, 32, 35 (top), 37, 39, 42, 43; AKG, London 7 (top), 24 (bottom), 34; Bridgeman Art Library/ Museum of Fine Arts, Houston, Texas 13/ Bibliotheque Mazarine, Paris, France 16/ Bibliotheque Municipale, Troyes, France 36/ Duomo, Florence, Italy 44/ Private Collection 45; British Library 15, 25, 35 (bottom); Corbis 40; Mary Evans 5, 38; Hodder Wayland Picture Library (title), 10, 11, 30, 33; Topham Picturepoint 24 (top)

Cover pictures: © Archivo Iconografico, S.A./CORBIS

LIBRARY OF CONGRESS CATALOGING-IN-PUBLICATION DATA

Woolf, Λlex.
    Education / by Alex Woolf.
        p. cm. — (Medieval realms)
Summary: Discusses the development of formal education during the Middle Ages, describing various methods of education, types of schools, curricula, who went to school, the rise of higher education, and more.
    ISBN 1-59018-532-3 (alk. paper)
    1. Education, Medieval—Europe—Juvenile literature. [1. Education, Medieval.] I. Title. II. Series.

    LA91.W85 2004
    370'.94'0902—dc22

                                            2003018309

Printed in China

Contents

Education in 1000

IN THE YEAR 1000 most people in Europe were uneducated, and could not read or write. Education was mainly offered to male children of wealthy or noble families. Even those who did receive an education generally left school at the age of fourteen.

At this time, Europe was just emerging from a period known as the **Dark Ages** when much of the **scholarship** of ancient Greece and Rome was lost. There were no universities in Europe in 1000, and what higher learning there was took place in monasteries, where monks continued to study the Latin works of ancient writers and **philosophers**.

The Church

Like most aspects of life in 1000, education was controlled by the Church. Schools were run by members of the **clergy**, such as bishops or priests, whose lessons followed the teachings of the Church. Few school buildings existed, and most classes took place in monasteries, cathedrals, and **parish churches**. Children did not study a wide variety of subjects, and most lessons were devoted to the learning of Latin grammar, reading and writing, and song.

Unlike today, education in 1000 was not seen as a necessary part of a child's upbringing. It was a path to be followed only by the sons of noble families selected for a career in the Church or in government service, where knowledge of reading and writing was essential. More rarely, girls from noble families were educated by nuns.

During the early Middle Ages, very few people, apart from monks, could read and write.

Aelfric (c. 955–1010)

Aelfric was a **Benedictine** monk who was regarded as the greatest Anglo-Saxon prose writer of his time. He became a monk at Cerne Abbas in Dorset before being appointed abbot of Eynsham in Oxfordshire. Aelfric's works included a book of sermons called *Catholic Homilies*, a summary of the first seven books of the Bible, and *Lives of the Saints*. He also wrote a Latin grammar book and a Latin-English glossary, used by many schoolchildren during this period. For this he was given the nickname Grammaticus.

Education was only for a chosen few, even among the **nobility**. For the great majority of nobles living in 1000, an understanding of the arts of war was seen as more important to a boy's development than **literacy** skills.

Informal Learning

Children from poorer backgrounds rarely had the opportunity to attend school. Most poor people lived in the countryside and worked on farms from an early age. Few would ever travel farther than a few miles from the village where they lived and would have had no use for reading and writing skills. Some might have learned about local history or heard about tales of other lands from the songs and stories of traveling **minstrels**. Often, they were taught by their parents or by attending church services and listening to sermons.

Latin

In 1000 Latin was the language of religion, culture, and learning throughout Europe, and it remains to this day the official language of the Church. In the **Middle Ages** it was the language of government, **diplomacy**, and serious literature. **Vernacular** languages (everyday languages of the people in a particular country) were rarely seen or used in written form, so to be literate in 1000 meant being able to read and write in Latin.

Minstrels traveled from town to town in the Middle Ages entertaining people with songs and stories of legendary heroes and the miracles of saints.

Education During the Dark Ages

IN THE FIFTH CENTURY, invading **Germanic** tribes defeated the **Western Roman Empire** and destroyed the civilized culture the Romans had created. For the previous four hundred years the Roman school system had provided state-funded education for many tribal leaders, public officials, and even craftsmen and traders living in Europe's urban centers. When the empire was defeated, this system fell into decline, and it disappeared entirely by the sixth century.

In the new **Barbarian kingdoms**, ancient learning and knowledge of Latin gradually died away. Only in the Church were efforts made to preserve the scholarship and literature of earlier civilizations. As Roman schools disappeared, the Church made efforts to establish schools of its own, and between the fifth and eighth centuries schools run by the clergy were set up in cathedrals, monasteries, and palaces.

Cathedral Schools

Schools founded by bishops and run by cathedral clergy were first set up between the fifth and eighth centuries. There were generally fewer than a hundred students in a school. Their original purpose was to train priests, but later they admitted **lay** (non-Church) students as well —usually boys of noble families being prepared for senior positions in the government.

Writing tablets and an inkwell from Roman times. Reading, writing, and arithmetic dominated the Roman school curriculum.

Ireland

During the fifth and sixth centuries Ireland became a famous center of learning. This was mainly due to the efforts of Ireland's patron saints, Patrick, Bridget, and Columba, who established schools in Armagh, Kildare, and Iona. These were followed by further schools, founded by Irish scholars, such as Clonmacnois, near Athlone. The reputation of these schools spread, attracting people from England, Scotland, France, and Germany. Many Irish scholars went to Europe to teach, found monasteries, and establish schools.

Some cathedral schools were organized as boarding schools in which trainee clergymen lived, studied, and worshiped together as a community. The most famous cathedral schools in the early Middle Ages (eighth and ninth centuries) were at York in England and at Orléans and Reims in France.

Monasteries

Monastic schools began as centers for the education of future monks. In time they opened their doors to students destined for the priesthood or government work. Monastic schools placed an emphasis on qualities such as duty, obedience, and humility. In the eighth century, the English monk Bede declared: "A child does not remain angry, he is not spiteful, does not contradict the professors, but receives with confidence what is taught him."

As well as providing schools for children, the monasteries were also the main centers of higher learning during the early Middle Ages. The first great scholarly monastery was founded at Monte Cassino in Italy in 529 by Benedict of Nursia. This inspired the development of many other Benedictine monasteries. By the eleventh century, thirty-five had been established in England alone.

Above: A cloister next to the church at the Abbey of Monte Cassino. The abbey was rebuilt after its destruction in 1943–1944.

Below: St. Benedict of Nursia. As a boy he attended schools in Rome. He gave up his literary studies at a young age to devote himself to God.

Benedict of Nursia (*c.* 480–547)

Benedict was born in Nursia, Kingdom of the Lombards, in northern Italy. As a young man he was shocked by the decadence of Rome, and went to live in a cave for three years. This austere lifestyle made him famous, and he was persuaded to become abbot of a nearby monastery. He later founded thirteen monasteries including the famous monastery at Cassino, halfway between Rome and Naples. Benedict laid down the rules for monasteries, which have been followed from that time on, including the provision of education. In 1964, Pope Paul VI proclaimed him the patron saint of all Europe.

Charlemagne

DURING THE EIGHTH and early ninth centuries, education underwent a revival in Europe. This was largely thanks to Charlemagne (*c.* 768–814), the king of the Franks (the present-day French), who was a great believer in the importance of education. When he became king he was shocked to discover that many members of the clergy did not have a good command of Latin. He ordered that lessons in Latin grammar, music, and the scriptures be made compulsory for all members of the Church. This program of forced education led to a new generation of clergymen with far higher standards of learning.

Above: This picture of the chapel at Charlemagne's palace at Aachen shows the emperor's throne. Charlemagne was passionate about education but was not himself a learned man.

Below: During his time as a teacher in York, Alcuin built up one of the finest libraries in Europe.

The Palace School

Charlemagne opened an advanced school at his palace in Aachen (now in Germany) where the best and brightest young **clerics** and lay people could study. To staff this school, and other centers of learning within his kingdom, he imported experts from different parts of Europe. English and Irish scholars

Alcuin (*c.* 740–804)

Alcuin was Europe's greatest scholar at the time of Charlemagne. He was an English poet, teacher, and clergyman. In 778 he became headmaster of the cathedral school of York, the most famous school of its day. In 781 he was invited by Charlemagne to become the head of his new palace school in Aachen. He reorganized the curriculum and raised educational standards. In 796 he became abbot of St. Martin at Tours, where he encouraged the development of a new style of handwriting known as the Carolingian minuscule. This script was more readable than previous scripts, and it soon spread throughout the empire.

introduced new subjects and methods of learning. Christians from Spain brought knowledge that they had picked up from Muslim scholars (the Muslim **Moors** controlled large parts of Spain at this time). From Italy came experts in Latin grammar and classical Roman traditions of teaching.

A Great Library

Charlemagne recognized the importance of books as a means of preserving and spreading knowledge, and he created a great library. Copies were made of books and texts from all over Europe, and added to the library. He also commanded that all schools have a scriptorium—a room set aside for scribes to copy out texts.

The Revival Spreads

Through his successes on the battlefield, Charlemagne expanded his territory, and by 800 he controlled not only France, but large parts of Christian Europe. In this powerful position he was able to spread his educational reforms over a far wider area. In 809 he decreed that every cathedral and monastery within his empire should establish a school to provide free education to every boy who had the intelligence and dedication to follow a course of study.

Charlemagne's reforms ensured the survival of traditions of education and scholarship at a time when European culture was in decline. He is regarded by many as the founder of medieval education.

A sample from the writings of Alcuin, the eighth-century scholar and teacher. Alcuin wrote several textbooks on subjects including arithmetic, geometry, and astronomy.

In 789 Charlemagne formalized the school curriculum. In the *Capitulary* of that year he decreed:

In every bishop's see [area under a bishop's authority], and in every monastery, instruction shall be given in the psalms, musical notation, chant, the computation [calculation] of years and seasons, and in grammar; and all books used shall be carefully corrected.

The Penguin Guide to Medieval Europe

The Role of the Church

MEDIEVAL EDUCATION was dominated by the Church. All schools, from the smallest classroom run by the village priest to Europe's top universities, were run by clergymen working within the authority of the Church. This dominance had developed gradually over a period of about five hundred years.

Beginnings

During the Church's early history, in the second and third centuries, the only schools in Europe were the grammar and **rhetoric** (speech and writing) schools of the Roman Empire. At this time, Christians were persecuted by Romans, and were not allowed to set up their own schools. Christian teaching was passed on informally within families and communities, by word of mouth. In 313, Christians were given the same rights as other citizens. They set up schools which gave Christian instruction to adults who wished to be baptized into the Christian faith.

By the time the Roman educational system collapsed in the sixth century, the Church had developed into a powerful organization. The various kingdoms that now ruled Europe lacked the administrative efficiency of the Roman Empire and this role was taken up in many cases by the Church. Bishops were often the only people with authority in local

Mirrors

As well as laying down rules for monks and clergymen, the medieval Church also offered a moral education to lay people. A series of religious texts written by senior churchmen between the fifth and eighth centuries, known as the mirrors, gave ordinary people guidance on how they should behave in their everyday lives. These texts were known as the mirrors because they held up the Christian Bible as the mirror in which men must learn to see themselves. They stressed the importance of the four moral virtues: prudence, courage, justice, and temperance (self-restraint).

Monasteries were centers of learning where chronicles and histories of medieval Europe were compiled.

A monk teaches boys destined to enter the Church. The Church ensured that the Bible remained the most important text in the classroom.

communities, and they frequently took over responsibility for education. Meanwhile, monasteries preserved the traditions of higher learning. Individual nations gradually won back political power from the Church, and the period between the eighth and fifteenth centuries can be seen as the struggle between Church and State for political power.

Official Education Provider

Under Charlemagne each cathedral and monastery was instructed to establish a school. But the Church's role as a provider of education was not made official until 1179. In that year a general council of the Church, known as the Third **Lateran Council**, decided to make it part of Church law.

It was in the Church's interests to control education. By doing so it was able to make sure that Christian teachings were passed on to the next generation, and that its power over people's hearts and minds was maintained. On a more practical level, the Church needed people who could read and write to fill the ranks of the clergy.

The control exercised by the Church over education reached its height between the twelfth and fifteenth centuries. During this period almost all of Europe's cultural and artistic achievements reflected the influence of the Church. There was general acceptance of the authority of the Church in all matters of moral life, belief, and behavior, including education.

Excerpt from *Canon 18* from the Third Lateran Council, 1179.

In order that the opportunity of learning to read and progress in study is not withdrawn from poor children who cannot be helped by the support of their parents, in every cathedral church a master is to be assigned some proper benefice [place to live] so that he may teach the clerics of that church and the poor scholars. Thus the needs of the teacher are to be supplied and the way to knowledge opened for learners.

Beliefs and Ideas in Education

SINCE MEDIEVAL EDUCATION was controlled by the Church, it naturally followed that the principles of education were based on Christian beliefs and ideas. In the Middle Ages, Christians believed that all knowledge and wisdom could be obtained from the study of great works, especially the Bible. Students were not encouraged to question this knowledge or to try to discover the truth for themselves. Their task was to read, learn, and interpret the truths already revealed.

Christian Beliefs in Teaching

Christian beliefs, and the interests of the Church, lay at the heart of all teaching. For example, arithmetic was taught so that students could calculate the dates of religious festivals. They were given singing lessons so that they could take part in church services. Most importantly, Latin was taught so that students could take part in church services and spread the teachings of the Church. Non-Christian Latin literature, such as the classical works of Roman writers, were sometimes used in the

A twelfth-century illustration of the Bible shows the story of Jonah and the whale. These stories were used in the classroom to teach children about how to lead a moral life.

Physical Education

Unlike the Greeks and Romans, who considered sporting activities to be an important part of education, the Church saw the human body as part of the unholy physical world and therefore something to be ignored or harshly disciplined. Schools tended to be cold and uncomfortable, and there was no organized physical activity. In 1423, an Italian teacher and physician named Vittore da Feltre began physical education classes for children— perhaps the first in a European school since ancient times.

classroom, but only as examples in the teaching of Latin grammar. These works were rarely studied for their content, except among a small number of scholars.

The Rise of the Sciences

By the late twelfth century, there was a growing interest in the sciences in European universities. By this time the works of ancient Greek scientists and scholars such as Euclid, Ptolemy, Hippocrates, and Galen were being rediscovered. During the Dark Ages, these works had been lost to Europe, but had been preserved by Muslim scholars, who had translated them into Arabic. By the twelfth century many of the Arabic **manuscripts** had been translated into Latin, and were finding their way back to Europe.

By this process, Greek ideas gradually filtered into medieval higher education, to be taught alongside the Christian teachings. Attempts were made by some medieval scholars to link Christian beliefs to Greek ideas about the universe. For example, the Greek philosopher Plato said there were five elements: earth, air, fire, water, and **quintessence**. Each of these elements held a place in the universe: earth elements were heavy, and therefore low, while fire elements were light, and therefore high. Medieval Christian scholars saw a connection between Plato's theory and their own beliefs about the sinfulness of the world and the purity of the heavens.

Through his writings, St. Thomas Aquinas helped to make the ideas of the Greek philosopher Aristotle available to medieval Europeans.

St. Thomas Aquinas (*c.* 1224–1274)

Thomas Aquinas was one of the greatest influences on medieval education. He attempted to bring together the two competing traditions of religious faith and rational thought. He believed that man's ability to reason was God-given and it was what placed him above the animals. However, faith was more important than reason, though both held an important place in education. His ideal was the scholastic, a man whose intelligence was balanced by his sense of morality and pious devotion to God. The scholastic ideal remained a guiding principle of medieval education.

Who Went to School?

FROM THE TIME of Charlemagne (768–814), the Church saw it as its duty to teach all children about religion and how to read and write. However, the vast majority of children in medieval times never went to school. There were two main reasons for this. First, in the Middle Ages, most people lived in the countryside, and their children were dependent on the local priest for any education they might receive. Many priests were not well educated themselves, and many others were simply lazy.

Second, poor people saw education as a luxury that only the rich could afford. They saw no point in their children learning how to read and write, when they could have little use for such skills in their later lives. Children were too valuable to their parents as a source of labor to have much time for education. As soon as they reached the age of seven, boys would go out with their fathers to work. They might learn to work on the farm or practice a craft or trade. Girls learned to run a household and become competent in skills such as embroidery. Country girls would also help with farm work. Their education, therefore, was purely practical, and designed only to meet the needs of their working lives.

Petrus Paulus Vergerius (1370–1444) was a teacher at Florence, Bologna, and Padua. He wrote the following about children and learning:

There is no doubt that nature has endowed some children with so keen, so ready an intelligence, that without serious effort they attain to a notable power of reasoning and conversing upon grave and lofty subjects, and by aid of right guidance and sound learning reach in manhood the highest distinction. On the other hand, children of modest powers demand even more attention, that their natural defects may be supplied by art [teaching]. But all alike must in those early years ... be inured [made used to] to the toil and effort of learning.

The New Education, c. 1400

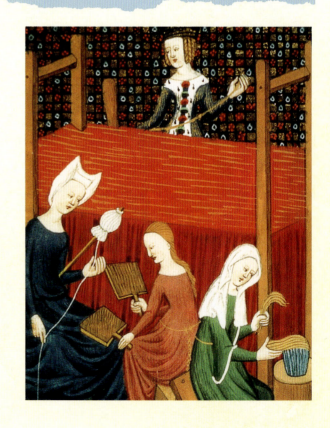

Few women attended school in medieval times. Instead they received a practical education in domestic skills, such as spinning and weaving.

Wealthy People

Even in richer families, by no means all children went to school. In many cases a tutor was hired to teach the children at home. Some noble families had their own priest who could give the children some literacy skills. But many noble families were suspicious of the benefits of education, and saw learning as less important than acquiring the skills of warfare. It was the custom of noble families to send their eldest sons to be trained in the arts of **chivalry** (see pages 28–29).

Those who attended schools were generally from wealthy backgrounds—the second sons of noble families, or the sons of lawyers, clergymen, small landowners, and merchants. Most of them were intended for a career in the clergy. Some older students were already ordained (appointed as priests). However, increasing numbers were aiming for a non-Church career, such as law and administration, for which knowledge of Latin was a requirement.

A child is taken to a monastery by his parents in this thirteenth-century illustration. Childhood did not last long in medieval times: at seven a child was regarded as being ready for either work or full-time study.

Literacy

To be literate in the Middle Ages, a person had to be able to read and write in Latin. For this reason, many of the nobility were classed as **illiterate**. Literacy was seen as a technical skill deemed more useful for the clerks that the nobility employed to read and write for them. Even some kings—including William the Conqueror and his son William Rufus—were illiterate. Writing was of less importance in a time when the king's **seal**—not his signature—was seen as proof of his authority.

What Did Children Learn at School?

FOR THOSE CHILDREN who went to school, their education normally began at the age of seven and ended at fourteen. After this they either began their careers or went on to study in schools of higher learning, which became known as universities.

There were many different kinds of schools in medieval times. These included small, informal schools held in the parish church; schools attached to cathedrals, such as song schools and grammar schools; schools run by monasteries, known as almonry or monastic schools; and commercial schools. The quality of education offered by any kind of school depended very much on the teacher in charge. In parish schools, for example, the level of education depended upon the attitude and abilities of the local priest.

Chantry Schools

Chantry chapels were set up by wealthy families to say masses for the souls of their founders and others. They had become common in the thirteenth century, and by the late fourteenth century were often also associated with schools. Chantry priests had no parish responsibilities (duties among the local population), and so founders might ask them to teach in addition to celebrating a daily mass. Others were not specifically asked to teach, but did so voluntarily to occupy their time. The colleges at Oxford and Cambridge began as chantry **foundations**, set up to teach as well as to pray for their founders.

Medieval teachers often asked children to sing the rules of Latin grammar as a way of memorizing them.

Early Learning

At all these schools Latin was at the center of the **curriculum**. It was learned first of all as a spoken language. Young children (seven-year-olds) commonly known as *parvuli* (Latin for young or little) or petties, might attend an ABC school where they would be taught to read Latin from a primer (a book used to teach children to read). They would learn the alphabet, followed by the main prayers and then the **psalms**.

When children first learned to read, the letters of the alphabet were introduced to them in the form of tiles. Each tile was three or four inches square and contained a different letter. This letter was colored in by the child, and then hung around the walls of the classroom.

Latin writing and grammar would usually only be taught when children were older than seven, and it was not taught at all at song schools (see pages 18–19). The other core subjects in the school curriculum were singing (learning and practicing of hymns and psalms) and the study of holy writ (the scriptures). Like Latin, both these subjects were necessary for taking part in church services.

Arithmetic

Some children—usually the sons of merchants or traders—were sent to commercial schools, where they were given instruction in arithmetic as well as Latin, both essential skills for anyone hoping to pursue a career in business. Commercial schools were set up by town authorities, such as in Lübeck, Brunswick, and Hamburg in Germany. However, most people aiming for a career in business learned arithmetic through an apprenticeship (see pages 30–31).

School Ends

For most people, education ceased at fourteen or fifteen. The more wealthy or gifted could go on to study the liberal arts at a university (see pages 34–35). For the rest, the basic instruction they had received in grammar and writing could lead to a career as a parish priest, or would be sufficient for a merchant, who could go on to acquire more specialized skills such as accounting during his apprenticeship.

A thirteenth-century illustration of a computist—a monk responsible for working out the dates of festivals in the Christian calendar. Good arithmetic was essential for such a job.

Song Schools

SINGING WAS REGARDED as a very important subject in medieval times, as it formed an essential part of all church services. Song schools had existed since the seventh century. They were set up by cathedrals to train people to become choristers (members of the cathedral choir).

Cathedrals ran several song schools in a city, based at the cathedral itself, and in other churches. Each song school was headed by a church official called a precentor. The precentor appointed deputies—succentors—to run each choir, and a songmaster to run each school.

The Gregorian Chant

The standard type of singing practiced in churches during the Middle Ages was known as the Gregorian chant, named after St. Gregory I, who was pope from 590 to 604. Members of the choir would sing in unison (sing the same notes together) following a strict set of rules. For example, one form of the chant, known as the sequence, had two-line verses, each with exactly the same number of syllables. The melody of the first line was repeated for the second line. A new melody was then introduced for the two lines of the second verse, before returning to the first melody for the third verse. An unlimited number of notes could be sung within each syllable. Under Charlemagne (*c.* 768–814), the

The nave of Notre Dame Cathedral in Reims, France. This beautiful thirteenth-century cathedral would have housed a song school to train its choir.

18

Gregorian chant became the dominant form of church music. It was as important a part of the service as the Latin scriptures and the prayers, and so song schools were just as important to the maintenance of church life as grammar schools.

Curriculum

Students at song schools were taught the **liturgical** chants. These were songs, such as hymns and psalms, to be used in church services. As well as singing, students were taught the alphabet, and how to read Latin religious texts, including the main prayers and psalms, though not necessarily to understand them. Students were not taught grammar, and had only a shallow, mechanical grasp of Latin—unless they also attended grammar school.

There were, however, song schools that offered a broader curriculum. Some of the song schools attached to the larger cathedrals and churches also taught grammar and writing. The song school at Canterbury even taught the sciences as they related to church services. For example, students studied how the seasons related to the religious year, and how to compose religious music and poetry.

A priest and several members of a choir sing liturgical psalms from the Bible.

In *The Prioress's Tale*, part of *The Canterbury Tales*, written by Geoffrey Chaucer between 1387 and 1400, the life of a young student at a song school is described:

This little child, his little lesson learning,
Sat at his primer in the school, and there,
While boys were taught the antiphons [hymns or psalms], kept turning,
And heard the Alma redemptoris [a hymn] fair,
And drew as near as ever he did dare,
Marking the words, remembering every note,
Until the first verse he could sing by rote [heart].
He knew not what this Latin meant to say,
Being so young and of such tender age....

He asks an older boy at the school to explain the Latin text, but the boy has only a vague idea:

"I can expound [explain] to you only so far;
I've learned the song; I know but small grammar."

The Canterbury Tales, The Prioress's Tale (a modernized version)

Grammar Schools

IN THE MIDDLE AGES, grammar always meant Latin grammar, as the grammar of vernacular languages had no formal rules in many cases until the fifteenth and sixteenth centuries. Schools teaching Latin grammar had been in existence since Roman times, although they remained few in number until the eleventh century. Like song schools, medieval grammar schools were set up and controlled by cathedrals, and were also known as cathedral schools.

The Rise of Grammar Schools

Many grammar schools were established during and after the **papacy** of Gregory VII (1073–1085), when all bishops were asked to see that the art of grammar was taught in their cathedrals. The Fourth Lateran Council of 1215 went even further by declaring that grammar school masters should be appointed not only in cathedrals but also in other churches that could afford it. By the 1300s most European towns and cities had at least one grammar school.

In England, French had been used in schoolrooms from the Norman conquest in 1066 until the fourteenth century when it began to be replaced by English. Some people mourned the loss of French in English schools. John of Trevisa (c. 1342–1402) was an English scholar who translated many Latin works into English. In 1385 he wrote:

The advantage [of English speaking in schools] is that they learn their grammar in less time ... the disadvantage is that now children at grammar school know no more French than does their left heel.

A Social History of Education in England

A fourteenth-century stone carving from Florence, Italy, shows grammar school students with a teacher.

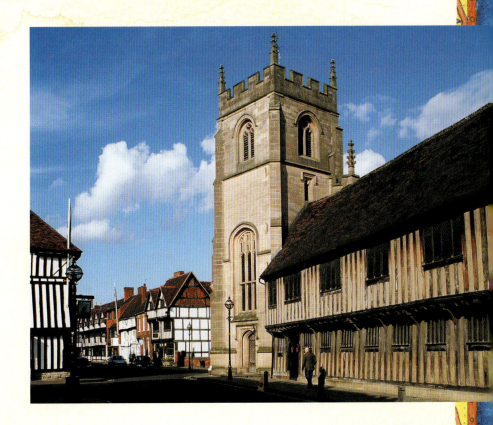

Not all grammar schools were run by the Church. Some, like this one in Stratford-upon-Avon, England, were set up by merchant guilds. Others were founded by town councils or hospitals.

Teaching Methods and Curriculum

The most commonly used textbook in medieval grammar schools was *Ars Minor* written by Aelius Donatus, which was an introduction to the parts of speech (rules of speaking and writing). Children were expected to learn this book by heart. Donatus, who lived in Rome in the fourth century, was the most famous Latin **grammarian** of his time, and his books were still used in schools over a thousand years after his death.

In most grammar schools, students progressed through a series of forms or grades. Promotion to a new form depended on ability more than age. The vernacular was used in teaching in the lower forms, until the child had made enough progress in the language for the whole lesson to be conducted in Latin.

Grammar schools varied in quality, but the number of teachers to students was low: many classes had upward of seventy students per schoolmaster. One school in Deventer, Holland, had two thousand boys spread over just eight forms!

The Later Middle Ages

Throughout the medieval period, grammar schools continued to offer a curriculum designed to train people for the clergy. However, by the fifteenth century, increasing numbers of students attended grammar schools with no intention of following a religious career. This can be shown by the fact that by this time about forty percent of London merchants could read some Latin.

School Buildings

Not many medieval grammar schools had their own purpose-built structures, and there are few examples still in existence in Europe. One can be found in the town of Wismar, Germany. It is a long, narrow, oblong brick building, typical of the architecture of public buildings of this time. School buildings from this time provided a large open hall and little else. More commonly, grammar schools operated from within other buildings, such as chapels or town halls. At Bristol and Oxford, teachers gave classes in rooms over the town gates or in their own houses.

Monastic Schools

MONASTERIES HAD BEEN seats of learning since the time of St. Benedict of Nursia in the sixth century (see page 7). Benedict had laid down a number of rules for monasteries, one of which stated that two hours each day should be spent reading. This began a tradition of study that led monasteries to become beacons of scholarship throughout the Dark Ages of the fifth to eighth centuries.

This role became less important from around the twelfth century as universities became the new centers of learning. The libraries of monasteries were semi-abandoned, used by only a few scholarly abbots. The monks, meanwhile, became more concerned with prayer and leading a life of self-discipline and self-denial, than with learning.

However, while their reputation for higher learning began to wane, monasteries continued to provide education for children throughout the Middle Ages. Monastic

A lesson is taught in a monastic school. Monks were taught that it is better to accept what you are told than to question it. They were also told that good behavior is more important than intelligence.

Teaching Methods

Pupils at monastic schools learned to write by spending several hours each day carefully copying out the Bible and other religious books. These copied works were then used to develop the monasteries' libraries. When not writing, pupils were often reading. As well as the two hours per day laid down by Benedict, students had additional reading time on Sundays and during Lent. They even had someone reading to them during mealtimes.

schools were originally established with the aim of educating **novice** monks, and this remained their main educational purpose, although by the tenth century lay students were also being admitted.

Novices

Novices tended to be drawn from local families. They were often the younger sons of **lesser nobility** or small landowners. They began their schooling at around seven years of age, and once they had completed their studies they were admitted into the monastery.

Until the establishment of cloister schools in the fourteenth century, novices' training tended to be focused on reading the scriptures, meditation, and prayer, with little intellectual content. This was a reflection of the general decline of scholarship in monasteries from around the twelfth century.

Almonry Schools

Lay students were offered a similar education to the novices. Until the thirteenth century, they were known as oblates (from the Latin *oblatus*, meaning one offered up). From the early fourteenth century, monasteries began opening grammar schools for lay people, known as almonry schools. These were supervised by the almoner (a person who distributed charitable donations to the needy on behalf of the monastery), and located near his house by the monastery's great gate.

Students of almonry schools received board and lodging and were taught Latin by a lay master. Almonry schools were small—about ten to twenty boys, who might be sons of wealthy tradesmen or farmers from the area. They would help in and around the monastery as partial payment for their education.

Cloister Schools

In 1335–1336, there was a move to broaden the education of novice monks when new standards were imposed by Pope Benedict XII. Each monastery was to have a cloister school where the novices—in groups of no more than five or six—would be taught the primitive sciences, meaning grammar, logic, and philosophy (see page 36).

A monk harvests wheat. A monastic education consisted of manual labor and prayer, as well as study.

School Life

ALTHOUGH SCHOOL LIFE for most children who went to school began at age seven and ended at fourteen, there were no strict rules about when people began or ended their schooling. Boys often left earlier or stayed longer according to their needs, while many simply dropped out.

Some schools had a series of forms, or grades, through which children gradually advanced. Others lumped children of different ages and abilities together, and it was not uncommon for a six-year-old to find himself sharing a bench with a sixteen-year-old. Classes at some of the larger schools could contain a hundred or more pupils.

A selection of medieval hornbooks. Young children of five or six often had one of these hanging from their waist so they could practice reciting the alphabet.

Reading and Writing Materials

In most medieval schools, teaching materials were scarce and of poor quality. A typical cathedral school might contain no more than about twelve books, all in the teacher's possession.

Writing was done using a bone or ivory **stylus** on wooden tablets coated with green or black wax. Parchment (a dried and treated animal hide used for books and documents) was rarely used. Paper was first developed in Europe in the thirteenth century, but did not become widely available until after the medieval period.

Books were all handwritten before the invention of printing in the 1450s, and were therefore very rare and expensive. Few medieval pupils would have had access to them.

Hornbooks

Most medieval schoolchildren learned to read from hornbooks. A hornbook was a wooden bat with a handle, and a **thong** to hang it up with when not being used. On the flat part of the bat, a page of text was glued, usually printed with the alphabet, letter combinations, and a religious passage. A thin layer of horn was laid over the top to protect the hornbook against wear and tear.

Teaching Methods

The teacher had a desk, and the pupils sat on the floor or on benches. Because of the lack of books and other materials, teaching was done almost entirely by word of mouth. The teacher lectured to the pupils, and then asked them about what they had learned. Some pupils took notes on a wax tablet, but most facts were learned through repeating them until the pupils had remembered them.

Grammar school students spent most of their mornings learning Latin by chanting. In the afternoons, they often studied passages of Latin poetry. Most school days lasted between ten and thirteen hours, with breaks for meals.

Discipline

Life at a medieval school could be tough, disciplined, and violent. Those who attended school were expected to work hard, and bad behavior was not tolerated. The teacher kept at his side a bundle of birch branches or rods as a symbol of his authority. If a student misbehaved, the teacher would select a branch and beat the child. No one was immune from punishment, young or old. One young man of nineteen or twenty, attending a school at Clitheroe in Yorkshire in 1283, was forced to leave school because he had been so badly beaten.

Guibert de Nogent (c. 1053–1124), abbot of Nogent-sous-Coucy, France, describes an incident that occurred during his schooldays:

I came and sat at my mother's knees. She, according to her wont, asked whether I had been beaten that day; and I, unwilling to betray master, denied it; whereupon, whether I would or not, she drew back my inner garment ... and found my little ribs black with the strokes of the osier [willow branch], and rising everywhere into weals [red, raised skin]. Then ... she cried, "Never now shall you become a clerk, nor shalt thou be thus tortured again to learn your letters!" Whereupon ... I replied, "Nay, even though I should die under the rod, I will not desist from learning my letters and becoming a clerk!"

Guibert de Nogent, *Own Life*.

Medieval schoolchildren were often beaten for bad behavior. They might have been punished for speaking in their own language, instead of in Latin.

Teachers

MOST SCHOOLMASTERS were low-ranked clergymen, and —certainly in the early Middle Ages—they were often poorly educated. This situation began to change in the latter half of the twelfth century, when teaching became more professional.

Teachers sometimes felt threatened by Church authorities, particularly when lecturing on subjects that appeared to challenge Christian teachings. In 1158 the teaching profession found its first protector, when Emperor Frederick I Barbarossa (1152–1190) of the Holy Roman Empire granted teachers certain rights and privileges under the law. They were given protection against unjust arrest, trial before their peers (somebody equal to their status), and permission to dwell in security. Later, these privileges were extended to include protection in financial dealings and the right to strike or discontinue lectures.

An illustration of a "magister" or teacher from a fourteenth-century manuscript. The most popular teachers could sometimes become more famous than their schools, and if they left, their students would often follow them.

Guibert de Nogent (*c.* 1053–1124), abbot of Nogent-sous-Coucy, France, describes his teacher:

This man therefore, to whom my mother was purposed to give me over, had begun to learn Grammar at an advanced age and was so much the more rude [unrefined] in that art, that he had known so little thereof in his youth. Yet he was of so great modesty that his honesty supplied his lack of learning.

Guibert de Nogent, *Own Life.*

The License to Teach

There were no formal qualifications required to be a teacher at this time, and it was up to a senior clergyman called a *scholasticus* to determine the applicant's fitness for the job. Schoolmasters could only teach within the limits of the city controlled by a *scholasticus*, who could then issue them a special license to teach called a *licencia docendi*. The city's clerical leaders would quickly intervene if anyone set themselves up as a teacher without a license. This system allowed the Church to maintain its control of the teaching profession and to ensure that all teachers remained loyal to the principles of the Church, while also allowing new schools to open in different parts of a city.

The reputations of the best teachers often spread to other cities, and it soon became apparent to the authorities that teachers should not be limited from practicing outside their home city. By the early 1200s, the *licencia docendi* had been replaced by the *jus ubique docendi*. This certificate was granted only after a formal examination, and it allowed teachers to work anywhere.

Specialist Teachers

With the development of higher education in the twelfth century, certain teachers became known for particular subjects, and students could specialize according to their tastes, by attending the classes of a particular master. For example, William of Champeaux at Paris was known for rhetoric and **theology**, and Bernard de Chartres for grammar.

Chartres Cathedral, southwest of Paris. The current building was begun in about 1145, some fifteen years after Bernard's death, and was completed in 1250.

Bernard de Chartres (died *c.* 1130)

Bernard de Chartres was a philosopher who became one of Europe's most famous teachers. From 1114 he taught grammar at the celebrated cathedral school of Chartres in northern France. He taught his students how to write Latin in four stages: first, they would read the text of a Latin author; second, they would analyze the text; third, they would imitate the text; and finally, they would undertake their own writing project.

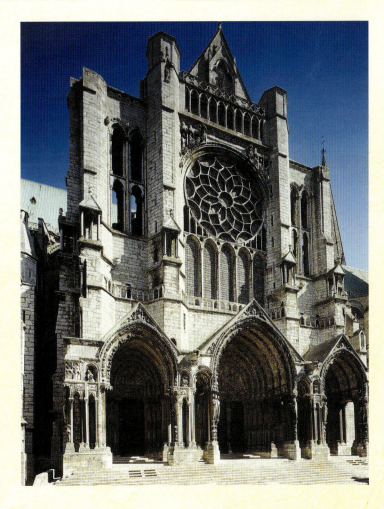

Chivalric Education

FOR THE MEDIEVAL NOBILITY, being a brave soldier was often held in greater regard than being a good scholar. Most noble families viewed the clergy or other scholarly professions as fitting for their younger sons. Eldest sons were more likely to become knights (warriors on horseback), fighting for their king or lord and receiving land in return.

Chivalry

To become a knight, a boy needed an education in chivalry—a special code which was supposed to govern the actions and behavior of every knight. Chivalry first developed in France around the late ninth century and reached the height of its popularity between about 1150 and 1350. Knights were

From *Little John of Saintré* by Antoine de la Sale (1388–1461), a French book on chivalry:

It is fitting that a knight's son be subject to his lord, and to this end, every knight ought to put his son in the household of another knight, that he may learn in his youth to carve at table and to serve, and to arm and attire [dress] a knight.

A Social History of Education in England

For the sons of the nobility, mastery of the arts of combat were regarded as very important. Here, boys are learning to wrestle and fight with swords. Meanwhile, girls learned to sew and spin wool.

expected to follow this code, which combined the military virtues of courage, endurance, loyalty, physical strength, and skill, with a romantic devotion to women and a duty to protect the poor and the weak. Knights were also expected to protect the Church from its enemies, which led many knights to take part in military expeditions called **crusades**, to recapture lands taken by Muslims.

The ideals of chivalry were reflected in the way knights were taught. There was a strong emphasis on physical education, hunting, **hawking**, horse riding, games, and how to use weapons. However, boys were also expected to learn how to behave at court. As well as learning how to behave courteously, they were taught how to dance, sing, recite poetry, and tell heroic tales.

Stages of Development

When the eldest son of a noble family reached the age of seven, it was the custom to send him away to the household of a great lord where he would learn how to become a knight. He began his education as a pageboy (personal servant to a knight), and learned how to read and write, sing and dance, play games, carve, and wait at table. He also learned the rules of heraldry (coats of arms and the symbols connected with them) and rank.

At around nine years of age, the trainee knight was ranked a valet, he was given a dagger and rode a horse, and learned battle skills from the **men-at-arms**. At fourteen or fifteen he was ready to serve as a squire, a knight's personal attendant in the castle and in the field. On reaching the position of squire, the young man was allowed to exchange his dagger for a sword, ride into battle, and learn firsthand about combat. At twenty-one the squire was ready to become a knight.

A squire kneels before the king and waits to be made a knight. He swore to uphold the knightly code, to protect the weak, defenseless, and helpless, and fight for the welfare of all.

Becoming a Knight

At around the age of twenty-one a squire would complete his training and be ready for knighthood. The squire would spend the day of his initiation in prayer and fasting. He would purify himself by confessing his sins and taking a ceremonial bath. The squire would then be dressed in a red robe and be brought before the king, who would dub [to honor somebody by giving them a new title] the knight with a sword on the shoulders and proclaim him "sir."

29

Apprenticeship

THE GREAT MAJORITY of children in the Middle Ages did not go to school. Most learned what skills they needed through their work, and that usually meant farming, since most people lived in the countryside.

For relatively well-off children living in towns—sons of city merchants, craftsmen, wealthy farmers, and the younger sons of nobles—a common form of education was apprenticeship. Apprentices would live and work with experienced craftsmen or traders, serving and assisting their masters in return for instruction.

The master would make an arrangement with the parents of the apprentice regarding the terms and period of apprenticeship. In the early Middle Ages, the period of training varied, but eventually it was set at seven years, from the age of fourteen to twenty-one. Masters were responsible for giving their apprentice board and lodging, clothing, and discipline, as well as instruction.

Apprenticeship contracts normally stated the term of years, salary, and promises of faithful work. This is an excerpt from a contract, dated April 13, 1248, between a barber and his apprentice, from Marseilles in France. An apprenticeship of two years, such as this one, was unusually short; most lasted four to seven years:

I, William, barber of Sestri, in good faith and without equivocation, place myself in your service and engage myself to work for you, Armand the barber, making my home with you, for learning the art or craft of barbering for a period of two years, at the salary or wage of forty solidi [gold coins] ... promising to be faithful to you in all things.

A Source Book for Medieval Economic History

A guildmaster supervises the work of a stonemason and a carpenter. To advance to the rank of master, a journeyman had to produce a masterpiece in his spare time.

This portrait depicts members of a guild of legal secretaries. As well as organizing the training of members, guilds also oversaw their moral education, and punished those who indulged in gambling or other bad behavior.

Basic Skills

The fact that most apprentices started at fourteen suggests that they already had some schooling. Indeed, some trades, such as stationers (makers of writing materials) and scriveners (people who made handwritten copies of documents, books, or other texts), required apprentices to have a basic level of literacy. Some high-ranking guilds (see panel), such as goldsmiths, forbade masters to take on apprentices who could not read or write.

All craftsmen required a certain level of literacy and numeracy in order to write letters and record sales and purchases, and this would form part of the apprentice's training. Some masters paid for their apprentice's schooling. In other cases, guilds recruited a teacher to tutor members' children, and perhaps their apprentices, in reading, writing, and arithmetic.

An apprenticeship was far more than a technical training; it was a preparation for life. Within the master's family, and the wider fellowship of the guild—with its worship, feasts, plays, and celebrations—they would gain much of their social and moral education.

Journeymen

At the age of twenty-one, apprentices would become journeymen. These were people who had completed their training, and could now be paid for their work, but who had not yet attained the rank of master. Journeymen often had to wait several years to achieve this status, as the number of masters in each guild was limited.

Guilds

Apprenticeship was normally organized through guilds. These were associations of people from the same trade or profession that developed between around 1250 and 1450. Guilds worked to protect their members' interests and maintain standards of skill and conduct. By overseeing the recruitment and training of apprentices, guilds ensured that these same standards were passed on to the next generation. Guilds made sure that apprentices received fair treatment, they oversaw standards of dress and behavior, and judged on cases of ill treatment.

The Education of Girls

GIRLS WERE FAR LESS likely than boys to receive formal education in medieval times. Girls from the lower social ranks—peasants or poor urban dwellers—were usually illiterate. From the age of about twelve, most girls from towns and cities were sent into service in other people's houses. In rural areas it was more common for girls to remain in the family home until they married, which usually occurred in their late teens or early twenties.

Girls from wealthier backgrounds would receive education in the home. From their mothers they would learn the creed (a formal summary of the principles of Christianity), the Paternoster (the Lord's Prayer), and the Ave Maria (a prayer also known as the Hail Mary). The three most important aspects of any girl's education were religious knowledge, manners, and household skills. The aim was to give them the skills they needed to blend into polite society and, when the time came, to make good wives.

A fourteenth-century illustration shows a poet-musician dictating one of his poems to a female scribe. Few women could read or write in medieval times. However, female scribes were sometimes employed by monasteries and nunneries.

The *Book of the Knight of La Tour-Landry* was written in 1371–1372 by Geoffroy de la Tour-Landry, a knight living in the province of Anjou, France. He wrote it as a book of instruction for his three daughters. This passage comes from the introduction:

I thought I would write this little book for my young daughters to read and study, so that by learning about good and evil in the past, they would stick to good and keep away from evil in the future.... And so I made my priests find examples in the Bible ... the histories of France, Greece, England, and many other strange lands. It is a great joy to find ways of steering [my daughters] towards goodness and worship, and towards loving and serving their creator, and towards loving their neighbours and the world.

Nunneries

Girls from rich families living in cities sometimes received instruction at the local nunnery. Like monasteries, nunneries were expected to educate their own novices, but they also offered board and lodging, and some schooling, to lay girls (and also boys), to help their finances.

Nuns were themselves not well educated, so the range of education they could offer would have been limited. Girls would learn the reading and singing necessary for church services, some Latin grammar, needlework, and embroidery. They may also have been taught some basic medical knowledge, such as the medicinal properties of different herbs. Higher education was not considered important or necessary for women.

Servants and Apprentices

Although few girls received book learning, many obtained a practical education as servants in other people's houses. Depending on where they worked, they would learn a whole range of household management skills, such as keeping accounts, minding a shop, running a dairy, or knowing the prices of different products. A few girls managed to secure an apprenticeship. Unlike servants, who could move from job to job, apprentices were bound to their employer for a period of about seven years during which time they would learn a craft such as embroidery or working in silk.

There were some women painters in the Middle Ages. In this fifteenth-century French painting a female artist is helped by her male apprentice.

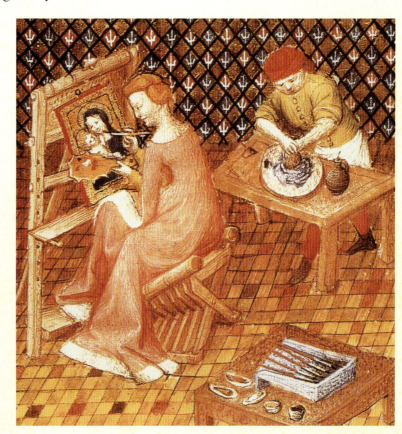

The Rise of Universities

DURING THE EARLY TWELFTH CENTURY, cathedral schools began to take over from monasteries as the main centers of scholarship. The authority and prestige of these schools was increased when they began to issue degrees, which were originally just licenses to teach, granted by the *scholasticus* (see page 27).

Studia Generalia

By the late twelfth century, a few great cathedral schools had acquired a reputation for excellent teaching, and had become well known across Europe. They were known as *studia generalia* —places where scholars from all parts may study or teach. Most importantly they were places that provided instruction beyond the range of subjects offered by most cathedral or monastic schools. They were the first centers of what we now call higher education.

The *studia generalia* included Orléans, Chartres, Laon, and Reims in France, Oxford in England, and Bologna in Italy. Degrees issued from *studia generalia*, known as *jus ubique docendi*, gave scholars the right to teach anywhere without further examination.

The Origin of Oxford University

Oxford was the first English university. It may have emerged out of a group of schools founded in the early twelfth century, but the real beginning came in 1167–1168 when a group of English students returned there from Paris, from which point on it became known as a *studium generale*. At this time it was essentially a community of masters and scholars, and remained so for the next century. The *studium* had no buildings of its own. Assemblies were held in the church of St. Mary, and masters rented rooms in nearby private houses to give lectures.

In the thirteenth century, rioting between the students and townspeople at Oxford led to the establishment of halls of residence for students, which became colleges. New College, pictured here, was founded in 1379.

In 1225, the title *studium generale* became formalized when Emperor Frederick II (1215–1250) officially conferred it upon the school of Naples. Pope Gregory IX did the same for Toulouse in 1229. The title was later granted to other famous European schools, such as the ones at Paris and Bologna in 1292. It soon became the rule that no school—with the exception of well-established *studia generalia* such as Oxford—could issue a universally valid teaching license without a license from a pope, emperor, or king.

The word *universitas* was originally used to mean the scholastic guild, or fellowship of masters and students, within the *studium*. By the second half of the fourteenth century, the term had come to mean an independent community of teachers and students officially recognized by a civil or church authority.

Masters and Students

At first, the organization of higher education was very informal, and the relationship between great teachers and their students was far more important than loyalty to any particular institution. The arrangement was in fact far more like that of an apprentice and master than that of a modern-day university student following a program of study.

Peter Abélard, the French scholar, and later, monk, wrote several religious and philosophical works, as well as a memoir, **The Story of My Troubles.**

Peter Abélard (1079–1142)

Born in Brittany, Abélard taught at Paris between 1108 and 1118, enjoying great renown as a teacher of rhetoric and logic (see page 36), and later theology. Lively and handsome, students flocked to him from all over Europe. Then in 1118 he fell in love with his student Héloïse, causing a scandal which destroyed his academic career. He spent several years as a monk before returning to teaching in 1136. He lived his final years at the abbey at Cluny.

Materials and resources were generally poor at medieval universities, with the only books belonging to the professors.

The University Curriculum

AT THE AGE of fourteen or fifteen, students could apply for a place at a *studium generale*, to study what were known as the **liberal arts**. These were seven subjects, inherited from the Roman educational system, split into two groups of three and four. The first group—the *trivium*—was made up of grammar, rhetoric (speaking and writing effectively), and logic (see box). The second group, called the *quadrivium*, was composed of geometry, arithmetic, music, and astronomy.

The liberal arts, as developed by the Romans, had ceased to be studied during the Dark Ages. Only grammar—and to a lesser extent, rhetoric—survived as school subjects during this period. Latin translations of the works of ancient Greek thinkers and scientists, such as Aristotle, Euclid, Ptolemy, Hippocrates, and Galen, led to a renewed interest in broader fields of scholarship, and the revival of the liberal arts.

A teacher gives a lesson in theology at the University of Paris. The university was originally set up in 1257 as a school of theology. By the early fourteenth century, there were around twenty thousand foreign students living in Paris.

Logic

Logic is a branch of **philosophy** that deals with the principles and structure of thought and reasoning. Logic gained in importance from the eleventh century—mainly because of a reawakening of interest in the works of Aristotle, and the influence of teachers such as Peter Abélard (see page 35) in Paris. Aristotle put forward the idea that every theory or belief had to be subjected to human reason before it could be regarded as true, and he invented a system of logic that could be used to judge any argument.

Vocational Subjects

Together the liberal arts provided a general foundation course—part practical and part academic—that had to be mastered before students could specialize in a subject that would train them for a career. The main vocational subjects (subjects relating to a particular career) were **canon** (church) law or civil law, medicine, and theology.

Theology was a long and difficult course, which took a minimum of eight years to complete—one could not be a teacher of theology in Paris before the age of thirty-five. Many students dropped out after only a year or two of study. As time went on more students turned to law and medicine because the courses were shorter and they were better-paid professions.

Philosophy

Those who preferred to pursue a life of scholarship could study philosophy, which was a very broad subject covering many of the topics already covered in the liberal arts, but in more depth. Topics included theology, physics, mathematics, grammar, rhetoric, and logic, as well as practical skills such as navigation, agriculture, and medicine.

Students of philosophy would specialize in a particular area depending on their tastes or the interests of their teacher. For example, William de Conches at Chartres was known for grammar and medicine; Thierry de Chartres for rhetoric; and Peter Abélard at Paris for logic and theology.

Petrus Paulus Vergerius was an early humanist and professor of rhetoric at Padua. In his book *The New Education* (*c.* 1400), he shows an obvious delight in certain subjects:

Arithmetic, which treats of the properties of numbers, Geometry, which treats of the properties of dimensions, lines, surfaces, and solid bodies, are weighty studies because they possess a peculiar element of certainty. The science of the Stars, their motions, magnitudes and distances, lifts us into the clear calm of the upper air.... The knowledge of Nature ... the laws and the properties of things in heaven and in earth ... this is a most delightful, and at the same time most profitable, study for youth.

A mid-fourteenth-century illustration depicts scholars with their books. Students were prepared to travel great distances to study the subject of their choice.

University Life

IN THEIR EARLIEST STAGES, universities were just associations for students and teachers. Discipline was relaxed and they were more like gatherings of enthusiasts for learning than formal institutions with rules and regulations. Universities in the modern sense, with officials, appointed teachers, and enrolled students, really only emerged in the mid–thirteenth century.

Bad Behavior

Even at this stage, students were unsupervised outside of teaching hours, left to find their own lodgings and lead their own lives. Many of the students, being no more than teenage boys, and virtually outside of adult control, could be badly behaved, noisy, and aggressive.

Conflicts between students from different countries were common. Jacques de Vitry (*c.* 1170–1240), who later became bishop of Acre, a port in the Middle East (in present-day northern Israel), was appalled when students in Paris began to

This illustration depicts Italian scholars and students in the fifteenth century. Some colleges offered free board and lodging to the poorest students.

Students without financial support from home could find life very hard. The following is part of a medieval song (possibly from the thirteenth century) in which a poor student is begging for money or assistance so that he can continue his studies:

**I, a wandering scholar lad,
Born for toil [hard work] and sadness,
Oftentimes am driven by Poverty to madness.
Literature and knowledge I Fain (with gladness)
would still be earning,
Were it not that want of pelf [money]
Makes me cease from learning.**

A Source Book of Mediaeval History: Documents Illustrative of European Life and Institutions from the German Invasions to the Renaissance

fight between themselves: "They impudently [disrespectfully] uttered all kinds of affronts and insults against one another."

Violence between students and citizens in a town was also common. After trouble flared between students and townspeople at Paris, Oxford, and Bologna, many universities set up a system of colleges. Colleges were schools or divisions within a university that were self-administered, and which provided food and accommodation for the students, teachers, and staff attached to them.

Types of University

By the fourteenth century, there were two types of university in Europe. The first originated with Paris and included English and central European universities. Here, the *universitas*, or guild of teachers, was responsible for discipline and academic standards. Officials appointed by the bishop were in overall control of the university, and teachers were paid by the cathedral authorities.

The other type of organization originated with Bologna, and was followed by Italian, Spanish, Scottish, and German universities. Here the student body was in charge, and elected the officials. Students hired their own professors and picked their own hours of study. They were free to leave one professor if they were not satisfied with him, and join another, attending several lectures before deciding whether to pay him or not.

Common to all universities by the fourteenth century were faculties, which were departments dealing with a particular subject. All the great universities had faculties of civil and church law, theology, and medicine.

A law lecture in progress at the University of Bologna. Although the university was founded in the eleventh century, it was based on a famous Roman law school established there in 425.

The Great Universities of Europe

THERE WERE SEVERAL great universities that began in Europe during the Middle Ages. These included the medical school at Salerno in Italy which had its origins in the ninth century; the university of Cambridge in England, which was begun by a group of Oxford students in 1209; and Valladolid in Spain, which obtained the rank of *studium generale* from Pope Martin V in 1418. Perhaps the three greatest universities of this period were at Bologna, Paris, and Oxford.

Bologna

A legal school was established at Bologna in 1088. The *studium generale* at Bologna was the result of students combining into an organized body at the end of the eleventh century and paying masters to lecture them. The masters formed their own guild later, at the end of the twelfth century. Around 1200 two new faculties of medicine and philosophy were added to the law school at Bologna, and a faculty of arts was added in the fourteenth century.

Paris

The first and most famous French university was the University of Paris, which grew out of the cathedral schools of the Notre-Dame de Paris in about the mid–twelfth century. It began as a guild of masters and students, and it grew to become a

A church at the University of Paris. The university was known as the Sorbonne, named after its founder, the theologian, Robert de Sorbon (1201–1274).

The University of Heidelberg

The oldest German university was established at Heidelberg. It was modeled on the University of Paris, and received its charter as a *studium generale* from Pope Urban VI in 1388. It contained five faculties: theology, canon law, medicine, the arts, and civil law. The university rapidly acquired a lasting reputation for great scholarship.

great center for teaching theology. By the end of the thirteenth century it was the most famous university in Europe, with professors including the English philosopher Alexander of Hales, and the great Italian philosopher and theologian Thomas Aquinas. It was divided into four faculties: theology, canon law, medicine, and the arts. Each faculty was divided into four student sections, each representing a different nation: French, Picard (from Picardy, a historical region of northern France), Norman, and English.

Oxford

The University of Paris became the model for French and northern European universities, including Oxford in England. The university came into being in the latter part of the twelfth century. In the thirteenth century, halls were established where students could live, and the first colleges were founded. The earliest colleges were University College (1249), Balliol (1263), and Merton (1264). By 1300, Oxford had fifteen hundred students, almost as large a number as there were townspeople, and there were frequent clashes between town and university. As its reputation for scholarship grew, the university attracted the support of the king, and it increasingly used this royal support to extend its power.

A map of Europe showing the development of universities in the Middle Ages.

The Rise of Humanism

HUMANISM WAS A philosophy that emerged in Italy in the fourteenth century, and later spread to other parts of Europe. It emphasized the development of human virtues, such as compassion and honor; and human potential, for example in education and the arts.

Humanists wished to transform the ignorant society of the Dark Ages into a new, more enlightened culture. Their main source of inspiration was classical literature—the recently translated works of Greek and Roman philosophy, rhetoric, and history. Through the writings of Plato, Aristotle, Cicero, and Livy, humanists discovered new ways of explaining the world, based on reason rather than religion.

Many of the early humanists were also deeply Christian, but they disagreed with the way medieval Christianity ignored human development and focused purely on the spiritual. They believed that ordinary human activities, such as education, business, and the arts, were also very important.

The rise of humanism coincided with social changes in Europe, especially the growth of commerce and the expansion of towns and

*This illustration is taken from a fifteenth-century French translation of Aristotle's **Ethics, Politics and Economics**. The book was one of many works that influenced the humanists.*

Petrus Paulus Vergerius was an early humanist and professor of rhetoric at Padua. *The New Education* (*c.* 1400) was a humanist blueprint for the future of education. In this passage he stresses the importance of books:

In [books] we see unfolded before us vast stores of knowledge, for our delight, it may be, or for our inspiration. In them are contained the records of the great achievements of men; the wonders of Nature; the works of Providence [the care and guidance believed to be provided by God] in the past, the key to her secrets of the future. And, most important of all, this Knowledge is not liable to decay.

cities. This would lead to the gradual transfer of political and economic power from the clergy and nobility to the wealthy city merchants and businessmen—the middle classes.

The new society that began to emerge around the fifteenth century required a different kind of education, based more on the everyday needs and activities of people. The rising middle classes tended to speak in the vernacular, leading to a rise in vernacular language teaching in schools in the 1400s, and a corresponding decline in Latin. This process was hastened by the invention of printing in the 1450s and the spread of books in vernacular languages (see box).

New Schools

Humanist schools, heavily influenced by classical Greek and Roman styles of education, were founded in several European cities in the fourteenth and fifteenth centuries. The humanist ideal in all things, including education, was balance and equilibrium (state of stability). In schools this meant education of the body as well as the spirit; and learning from discussion, as well as from private reading. Humanists also believed that education was not something confined to what one learned at school, but was a process that continued throughout life.

However, this humanist revolution in education did not extend itself to the great mass of the population, but was limited mostly to the sons of royalty, nobility, and wealthy merchants.

Printing

The invention of printing in Europe, by Johannes Gutenberg, between 1440 and 1450, had a profound effect on the world of education. Suddenly it was possible to mass-produce written materials. Books, instead of being in the possession of a few learned scholars, were available to students and teachers alike. University libraries expanded from fewer than a hundred volumes to many hundreds. The learning of scholars in Bologna could be transmitted to those in Oxford, Paris, or Valladolid in a much shorter space of time. Literacy levels rose as access to literature increased, spreading beyond the clergy to the emerging middle class.

The first printing press in Florence dated from the late fifteenth century. As well as printing in Latin, the new presses printed books in national languages. This contributed to the decline of Latin as the main language of Europe.

The Spread of Humanism

HUMANISM WAS THE underlying philosophy behind the Renaissance, which began in Italy in the latter half of the fourteenth century. The Renaissance (meaning rebirth) was a period in European history lasting until the sixteenth century, which marked the end of the Middle Ages and featured major artistic and cultural changes.

Platonic Academy

During the Renaissance, centers of humanist learning opened in Italy in the second half of the fifteenth century. The first was the Platonic Academy, established in Florence, and inspired by the Academy of the ancient Greek philosopher, Plato. Similar academies soon opened in Rome and Naples.

Marsilio Ficino (1433–1499) was a famous humanist scholar who taught at the Platonic Academy in Florence.

Gymnasia

As part of the enthusiasm for all things Greek, which characterized the Renaissance, new schools were established called *gymnasia*—the name used for schools in ancient Greece. They were set up by the ruling families of many major cities for the humanist education of young aristocratic boys.

Students were given an introduction to the liberal arts in preparation for university life. At the Venice and Ferrara *gymnasia*, both set up by the humanist scholar Guarino

Vittore da Feltre (1378–1446)

The Italian educator da Feltre is often regarded as the greatest humanist schoolmaster of the Renaissance. After twenty years as a student and teacher at the University of Padua, Vittore set up a new school, La Giocosa (The House of Joy) in 1423. There were about sixty pupils from royal and noble families, plus poor boys chosen for their ability. They studied Greek, Latin, arithmetic, geometry, and music, as well as games and physical exercises. He was known as a caring teacher, who adapted his methods to suit each child's abilities. There was no **corporal punishment**. La Giocosa was possibly Europe's first boarding school.

Veronese (1374–1460), studies were organized into three stages: the elementary stage, when reading and pronunciation were taught; the grammatical level; and finally the highest level, which concentrated on rhetoric.

Humanism Beyond Italy

In other parts of Europe—mainly England, Holland, France, and Spain—humanism also brought about educational reform, but more slowly than in Italy. In Holland, a humanist group known as the Brethren of the Common Life established hostels for students in the fourteenth century, and, later, schools in various Dutch cities.

Humanism also flowered in late-fifteenth-century England, where a number of new educational institutions were founded. John Colet founded St. Paul's School in 1510, the first of a new type of grammar school, based on humanist principles.

Changes in Education

Education in Europe underwent major changes between 1000 and 1500. Learning was no longer confined to the monasteries, but had spread to a great number of the upper and middle classes. Teaching had become more professional, and the Church was losing its control over the curriculum. The reemergence of ancient Greek scholarship, the rise of the universities, the expansion of trade and commerce, and the invention of printing, had all influenced the quality and increased the breadth of education by the end of the Middle Ages.

Desiderius Erasmus (c. 1466–1536), the Dutch humanist and scholar, was one of the most influential figures of the Renaissance. He studied and taught at Paris and Oxford.

Chronology

c. 313	From this date, Christians begin to set up catechetical schools.
476	Deposition of last Roman Emperor in the West; Europe is invaded by German tribes.
529	Monastery at Monte Cassino is founded by Benedict of Nursia.
c. 550	Roman school system has disappeared.
c. 650–850	Irish scholars go to Europe to teach, found monasteries, and establish schools.
781	Alcuin is invited by Charlemagne to become head of the palace school at Aachen.
789	Charlemagne formalizes the Frankish school curriculum.
796	Monks at St. Martin at Tours begin to develop a new style of script—the Carolingian minuscule.
809	Charlemagne decrees that every cathedral and monastery within the Holy Roman Empire should establish a school.
c. 1000	Aelfric writes his Latin grammar and Latin-English glossary, used by many schoolchildren in this period and after.
1073	Many grammar schools are established from this date.
c. 1088	A legal school is established at Bologna.
1100s	Works of ancient Greek scholarship are translated from Arabic into Latin, and find their way back into Europe.
1150s	The first *studia generalia* emerge at Paris and Bologna.
1158	Holy Roman Emperor Frederick I Barbarossa grants teachers certain rights and privileges.
1167–1168	*Studium generale* at Oxford is founded.
1179	Third Lateran Council: 1) Church's role as a provider of education is made part of church law. 2) Only those with a *licencia docendi*, granted by a *scholasticus*, are permitted to teach.
1200s	*Licencia docendi* replaced by *jus ubique docendi*, giving teachers the right to work anywhere.
1209	*Studium generale* at Cambridge is founded.
1215	Fourth Lateran Council decrees that grammar school masters should be appointed in any church that can afford it.
1225	The term *studium generale* is formalized when Emperor Frederick II confers it on the school of Naples.
1259–1273	Thomas Aquinas writes his two greatest works, *Summa contra Gentiles* and *Summa Theologiae*.
1292	Schools at Paris and Bologna are formally given the titles of *studia generalia*.
1300	By this date, most European towns and cities have at least one grammar school.
1300s	Monasteries begin opening almonry schools—grammar schools for lay people.
1335–1336	Pope Benedict XII declares that all monasteries should open a cloister school for its novices, to teach them about grammar, logic, and philosophy.
1368	Heidelberg University is founded.
1396	Manuel Chrysoloras helps to popularize the study of the ancient Greek language and culture in Europe.
c. 1400	Humanist teacher Petrus Paulus Vergerius writes his book, *The New Education*.
1408	The first *gymnasium* is established at Padua, Italy.
1423	Vittore da Feltre founds a revolutionary school, La Giocosa, in Padua, Italy.
1440–1450	Printing is invented in Europe.
c. 1450	The Platonic Academy is founded in Florence, Italy.
1510	John Colet founds St. Paul's School, the first of a new type of grammar school, based on humanist principles.

For Further Research

Richard Barber, ed., *The Penguin Guide to Medieval Europe*. New York: Penguin, 1984.

Europe in the Fourteenth and Fifteenth Centuries. Harlow, Essex, UK: Longman, 1989.

John Lawson and Harold Silver, *A Social History of Education in England*. London: Methuen, 1973.

A Source Book for Medieval Economic History. Milwaukee, WI: Bruce, 1936; reprinted New York: Biblo & Tannen, 1965.

A Source Book of Mediaeval History: Documents Illustrative of European Life and Institutions from the German Invasions to the Renaissance. New York: Cooper Square, 1972.

Glossary

abbess   The nun in charge of a convent.

Barbarian kingdoms   States ruled by invading tribes who took over the territories controlled by the Roman Empire.

Benedictine   Relating to the monastic order founded by St. Benedict.

canon   A member of the clergy who helps in the running of a cathedral.

chivalry   The code of honor that a medieval knight was expected to follow.

clergy   The body of people qualified to give religious services in a church.

cleric   A qualified priest.

corporal punishment   The striking of someone as punishment.

crusades   Military expeditions made by European Christians between the eleventh and fifteenth centuries to reconquer areas captured by Muslim forces.

curriculum   The subjects taught at an educational institution such as a school or university.

Dark Ages   The period of European history between the fall of the Roman Empire in 476 and about 1000, during which life was comparatively uncivilized.

diplomacy   Management of the relationships and communications between the governments of different nations.

foundations   Institutions that have been set up by means of an endowment fund (an income or property donated by a person, family, or institution).

Germanic   Something or somebody from Germany.

grammarian   A writer on grammar.

hawking   Hunting animals with a trained hawk.

illiterate   Unable to read or write.

Lateran Council   Meetings of Church leaders, held at the Lateran Palace in Rome, to discuss Church policy. There were five Lateran Councils altogether, taking place between the twelfth and sixteenth centuries.

lay   Relating to people who belong to a church, but are not members of the clergy.

lesser nobility   The lower ranks of the nobility, such as baronets, knights, and viscounts.

liberal arts   The seven subjects of medieval higher education: grammar, rhetoric, logic, geometry, arithmetic, music, and astronomy.

literacy   The ability to read and write.

liturgical   Relating to the liturgy, which is the form of public worship laid down by the Church.

manuscripts   Books written by hand.

men-at-arms   Armed soldiers.

Middle Ages   The period in European history between the fall of the Roman Empire and the Renaissance.

minstrels   Medieval singers, musicians, or reciters of poetry who traveled from place to place giving performances.

Moors   People of Arab or Berber descent who originally occupied various parts of North Africa and Spain.

nobility   A high-ranking class of people in a country, who achieved their status through birth.

novice   Somebody who has joined a religious order but has not yet taken the final vows of a monk or nun.

papacy   The period of office of a pope.

parish church   The church within a parish; a parish being an area that is under the authority of one priest.

philosopher   Somebody who seeks to understand and explain the nature of life and reality.

philosophy   A form of study that is devoted to examination of concepts such as truth, existence, reality, and freedom.

psalms   Sacred songs or poems of praise.

quintessence   The fifth and highest element in ancient and medieval philosophy that was believed to form the stars and sun and to be present in all of nature.

rhetoric   The study of methods used to write or speak effectively and persuasively.

scholarship   Another word for learning.

seal   A ring or stamp with a raised or engraved symbol that is pressed into wax in order to make a document official.

stylus   A pointed instrument used for engraving.

theology   The study of the Christian faith and God's relation to the world.

thong   A thin strip of leather used for fastening or hanging something.

vernacular   The everyday language of the people in a particular country or region.

ward   A young person who is under the care of a guardian.

warden   Somebody in charge of an institution such as a school or college.

Western Roman Empire   The western part of the Roman Empire which was divided into two empires in 395. The Western Empire fell to barbarian invaders in 476.

Index